WHAT DRIVES WINNING
ENVIRONMENTS

BY BRETT LEDBETTER

© 2020 by Brett Ledbetter. All rights reserved.

No part of this book may be used or reproduced in any manner whatsoever without the written permission of the publisher.

Printed in the United States of America

Books may be purchased in quantity and/or special sales by contacting What Drives Winning at info@whatdriveswinning.com or visiting WhatDrivesWinning.com.

Library of Congress In-Publication data has been applied for.

ISBN: 978-0-9962264-3-1

Cover and interior design by Lisa Kuntz

FIRST EDITION

10 9 8 7 6 5 4 3 2

TABLE OF CONTENTS

7 OVERVIEW

9   The Goal of This Book

11   Define | Manage | Model

21 DEFINE

23   How U: Draw the Line

35   Define Road Map

41 MANAGE

43   Catching Above-the-Line Behavior

63   Converting Below-the-Line Behavior

81 MODEL

83   Representing the Standard

99   Model Road Map

101 AUTHOR'S NOTE

OVERVIEW

The Goal of This Book

To stimulate thought around this question:
How do I build an environment where people can do their best work?

DEFINE | MANAGE | MODEL

What's the difference between character development and behavior management?

Take a second to think about how you would answer that question. When I ask coaches that question, their response goes something like this, "Character development is the long game. Behavior management is right now."

Then I ask, "Which one is more important?" Which one do you think coaches choose? Most say, "The long game."

Here's what I've found: the *moment* is where trust is earned or lost. If you don't have trust with your players, it's hard to shape who they become as people. In other words, if you don't win the *right now*, it's hard to win the *long game*.

I think that's why I prefer the word "environment" to "culture." Environment is *right now* and culture is the *long game*. Culture becomes the by-product of the day-to-day environment over time.

When an NBA general manager was asked about his role in the organization, he responded, "To build an environment where people can do their best work."

How do you do that? When I ask coaches, it usually comes down to three things: How you **Define**, **Manage**, and **Model** your expectations.

Defining expectations is a proactive approach (before something happens).
Managing expectations is a reactive approach (after something happens).
Modeling expectations is all the time (constant).

I'm going to provide a quick overview for each of these components before we take a deep dive into each section. Let's take a closer look at how this three-pronged behavior management system works.

DEFINE

What do you think about this quote from the first man on the moon, Neil Armstrong? "If you're an inch off on landing, no big deal. If you're an inch off on takeoff, you miss the moon by a million miles."

How does that apply to teams?

An athletic director challenged me to find a video that captures the meaning of that quote. The video that came to mind was a Pop Warner football team playing their first-ever game.

It showed a young football team just learning how to play the game. Right before game time, they were going to make an entrance by running through a banner with cheerleaders on the other side.

As they started running, something happened. Confusion set in and they didn't know which way to run through the banner.

The player leading the charge fell, which set the team into chaos. Half the group picked one side. Half the group picked the other. And they met in the middle with an unexpected collision:

If there was a graphic representation of what that youth football team looked like, it might be this:

Everybody's going in their own direction. Have you been on a team like that? What does that feel like?

Compare that to this professional pit crew:

Within five seconds, the race car is ready for action. Take a look at that picture and think about these questions:

- How many people are in the picture?
- Does everybody have a role?
- Does every role matter?
- Are there guidelines painted on the pavement?

What does the graphic representation of the pit crew look like?

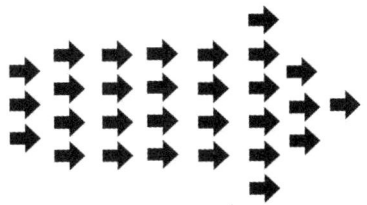

The difference between the two is clear.

Everybody on the pit crew is on the same page. That's what Defining is. It's drawing a line between what's acceptable and what isn't.

WHAT DRIVES WINNING ENVIRONMENTS 13

In the Define section of this book, we'll look at creative ways that elite coaches have effectively taught what they expect.

MANAGE

The Gonzaga men's basketball team was losing at halftime to a less talented team, 31–22. In the second half, they came back to win by 17. The final score was 71–54.

After the game, the announcers asked Gonzaga's head coach, Mark Few, "What did you say to your team at halftime?"

Mark responded, "Be us. That was not us. You're doing things I haven't seen in practice."

What's Mark doing? He's coaching to an identity: "Be us." What's the hardest part about being us? Knowing what "us" is and what it is not.

That's why Gonzaga's head strength coach, Travis Knight, spends every Monday with the team on PGMs (Personal Growth Mondays). Part of the curriculum: Identity Formation.

We asked the group, "What does that term mean to you?" Everybody wrote down their answers, and after a few minutes we talked through their responses. We landed on, "Developing who you are as a team."

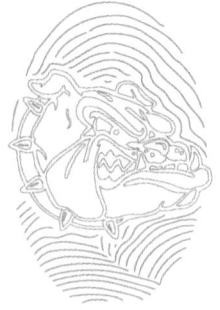

Here's a symbol of how Gonzaga approaches that:

In the middle of the thumbprint is their logo. Everybody in the basketball world knows the Gonzaga brand that has been built over the last two decades. The challenge for each team is to put its unique DNA on the program. Hence the thumbprint.

Just like an iPhone captures the details of your thumbprint in segments and it doesn't form all at once—that's how each team's identity is formed. That resonated with Travis and the team. They form their identity throughout the year together.

Here's an example of how they illustrate their identity as a team. Travis showed the team a clip of the conference player of the year getting emotional after a referee's call:

After he showed the team that clip, he showed this:

It featured the same player diving on the floor for a loose ball.

This is in character. When he gets up, his team rallies around his blue-collar work ethic.

What's Travis doing? He's delineating the difference of who they are when they're in character versus who they are when they aren't.

Travis uses imagery to make the point:

That's what Managing is about. It's about catching above-the-line behavior, which is what wins. And it's about converting below-the-line behavior, which is what loses.

In the Managing section, we'll dive into a professional approach on how to catch and convert behavior. We'll also look at how to get you started with developing a behavioral playbook that works for you.

MODEL

As a coach, you're constantly sending signals to your staff and team. Those signals either align with your expectations or they don't.

When they don't, you're sending mixed signals. What does that look like?

There's an incredible clip from the movie *Old School*. At halftime, Will Ferrell's character loses his mind:

He's screaming, "We can't have anyone freak out out there. We've got to keep our composure! We've come too far! There's too much to lose—we've just got to keep our composure!"

As he's screaming, he's beating a chair against the lockers. Look at how the rest of the team is looking at him:

It's beautiful imagery; he's the emperor with no clothes. His words are in direct conflict with his actions in this exact moment. He's hysterical, yelling, "We've got to keep our composure!" That's the definition of a mixed signal. The goal in modeling: Eliminate mixed signals. How do you do that? Consistency.

Bill Belichick, the New England Patriots football coach, is the model for consistency. Here's an exchange between Bill Belichick and a reporter:

Bill Belichick
New England Patriots

Reporter: *With all you've accomplished in your coaching career, what is left that you still want to accomplish?*

Belichick: *I'd like to go out and have a good practice today. That would be at the top of the list right now.*

That's what a seasoned vet sounds like.

I showed that interaction to Mike Holder, who's the athletic director at Oklahoma State. Mike had a great response, "If I want my team to be in the moment, then I need to be in the moment."

I started to think about Mike's response. What happens if you underline "be in the moment"?

> **If I want my team to be in the moment**
>
> **then I need to be in the moment**

There's a great modeling tool that can grow from that, and extends to just about any behavioral model:

> **If I want my team to (fill in the blank)**
>
> **then I need to (fill in the blank)**

Mike Holder has always said, "You are the physical manifestation of your standard."

One of the best lessons that I learned about modeling came from something that we did with the Gonzaga men's basketball team. I asked them, "What's the best lesson that you've learned from Mark Few?"

The number-one answer that came up was, "How to be a good husband and good father."

I asked Mark, "How many conversations have you had with the team about those topics?"

Mark's answer, "None."

Which shows us what? Most of the lessons that people learn from us are caught with their eyes, not heard with their ears.

In the Modeling section, we'll look at how to eliminate mixed signals and develop a game plan that allows you to have an authentic approach toward your team.

IN SHORT

The goal of this book is to get you to consider how you can build an environment where people can do their best work.

And when things get off track and don't go as planned, we hope you can develop a countermove, which you can discover by self-auditing and using these three questions:

1.) Have I defined it well?
2.) Have I managed it well?
3.) Have I modeled it well?

DEFINE

HOW U: DRAW THE LINE

If I asked you who the best NFL coach is, who would come to mind?

When I ask football coaches, it's an easy answer: Bill Belichick. He shared something with me that I showed a group of kindergarten teachers that really resonated with them:

Bill Belichick
New England Patriots

A player can't overcome bad coaching. If you don't teach them the right way to do things, then it's hard for them to do them right.

So it's important for the coaches to give the players a good plan, a good level of instruction, and an opportunity to be able to go and perform and execute their job.

If you teach them that, then you have a chance for that to happen. If you don't teach it to them, then I'd say the chances of a player getting that on his own, and just totally figuring it out without much help, is putting a lot of pressure on the player.

A coach has to do his job and teach the information and the concepts in a way the players can comprehend them and execute them.

Bill is coaching at the highest level. Why do you think that resonated so much with kindergarten teachers? Take a look at what they have to teach their students before they can even begin with the curriculum (next page).

WHAT I LEARNED IN KINDERGARTEN...

1. How to walk in a line
2. How to raise your hand
3. How to sit on the floor during circle time
4. How to walk down the hall without talking
5. How to not look under the stalls in the bathroom
6. How to not jump up and touch hallway decorations
7. How many pumps of soap you need to wash your hands
8. How to wash your hands
9. How to put your straw in your milk
10. How to carry a tray in the cafeteria
11. How to throw away your own trash
12. How to listen
13. How to wait your turn
14. How to write your name
15. How to recognize feelings
16. How to talk through your feelings
17. How to play well with others
18. How to be a helper
19. How to hold a pencil
20. How to cut with scissors
21. How to button your pants
22. How to blow your nose
23. How to open your snack
24. How to look at someone when they are speaking to you
25. How to use glue
26. How to clean up your mess
27. What to do when you lose a tooth
28. How to keep your hands and feet to yourself
29. How to sit in a chair
30. How to ask for help
31. How to drink out of the water fountain
32. How to have appropriate touch
33. How to be a friend
34. How to share

Bill said, "If you don't teach them the right way to do things, it's hard for them to do things right."

The same goes for kindergarten teachers. If you don't specify, say, to use only two pumps of soap when washing your hands, you'll end up with a soap war. If you don't clarify scissors are only used for paper, somebody will give themselves (or a friend) a haircut.

Take a look back at the kindergarten list. What does every line start with? It starts with the word "How." Coaches must teach the information and concepts in a way the players can comprehend and execute.

Maybe that's why Neil Armstrong's quote resonates so much with football coaches:

"If you're an inch off on landing, no big deal. If you're an inch off on takeoff, you'll miss the moon by a million miles."

It certainly resonated with P.J. Fleck, who coaches football at the University of Minnesota. In the 2019–20 season, Minnesota finished ranked in the top ten. The other nine schools had 30 or more four- and five-star recruits. Minnesota had four. That shows that P.J. has been able to do more with less "talent."

P.J. used to be a fifth-grade teacher. He learned something from that experience that he credits to his football team's success. It's called "How University" or "How U."

How University is where anything that is expected is defined. P.J. closes the gap of interpretation to get everybody on the same page.

Tim Corbin, the Vanderbilt head baseball coach, does something similar to what P.J. does. Check this out. This tweet went viral right after Vanderbilt won the National Championship in 2019: →

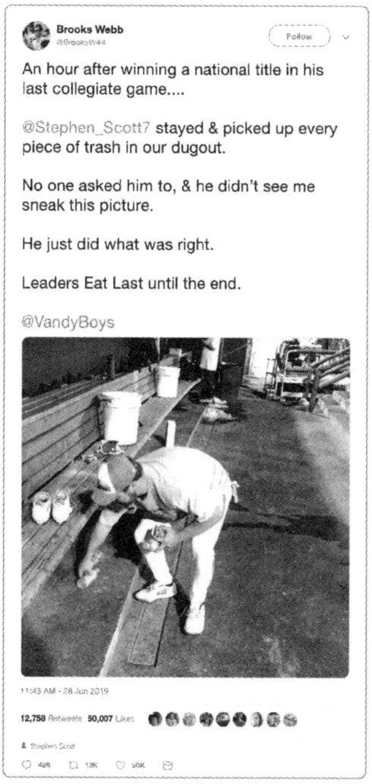

Here's what's cool: each day the baseball team has a classroom session led by their head coach before they hit the field.

Here's one of the lessons:

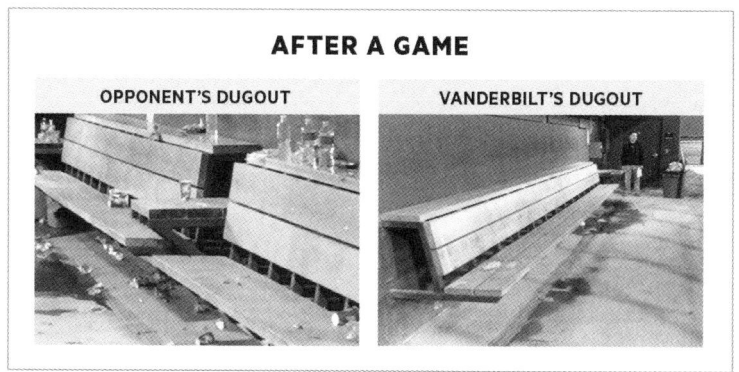

AFTER A GAME

OPPONENT'S DUGOUT | VANDERBILT'S DUGOUT

WHAT DRIVES WINNING ENVIRONMENTS   25

That's trained behavior. It doesn't happen by chance.

Tim lays the foundation at the beginning of each year. He explains what happens during the first meeting of the year with the team:

Tim Corbin
Vanderbilt

It's an hour and fifteen minutes. And I don't speak about baseball one time.

He doesn't speak about baseball once. That reminds me of the kindergarten list. They're laying a foundation.

Which is why Tim shows this picture on the left to the team:

He then puts up this picture right next to it:

By the end of the year, they're going to build something beautiful together. Each day the team builds on that foundation.

Most coaches check the box with their first meeting and expect it to happen. Tim doesn't. He communicates how the process is going to work.

If productivity matches the clarity of direction, here's the clarity with which Tim communicates:

A few years ago, I observed a classroom session. It was their Fall Cleaning Day, and it was one of the best lessons in teaching I've ever seen. The team was going to clean their facility before they left for Christmas break.

Tim flashed this on the screen:

It was each of the spaces that needed to be cleaned, and groups of three to four were assigned to each one (staff was included).

Once everyone knew which space they were responsible for, Tim showed this:

People might look at this and think it's a lesson on how to clean. Others understand that this is about communication. It's about closing the gap of interpretation and clearly defining what you expect.

He takes the same approach with behavior.

I observed another classroom session the day after the team had a poor practice. Tim addressed it by reminding them of who they are.

He showed the team this picture:

He asked, "What do you see when you look at this?" He paused, then asked, "Are they ready for battle?"

"Head down. Sloppy. Everybody going in their own direction. How many of you have played teams like this?"

Everyone raised their hands.

He added in, "That's who we were yesterday."

He then showed this picture:

He asked, "What do you see?" After pausing, "Are they ready for battle?"

"Where did they learn that from?" The team answered, "Each other."

Tim is using imagery to draw a line to show the team what it looks like when they're in character and when they aren't: →

Tim ended the meeting by saying, "We lost yesterday. We disrespected our environment. If I know this team like I think I do, I know how you all will respond."

When you have an identity, you have standards to live up to that can help create a sense of ownership, which in turn draws clear lines of accountability.

Mike Krzyzewski, head basketball coach at Duke University, had a valuable experience using the team's input to create standards. He has come to understand how asking questions can increase the players' sense of ownership and responsibility. I asked him about the importance of questions:

Mike Krzyzewski
Duke

It produces discussion. It gives them ownership. If you tell them the answer before you ask the question, it may only be your answer. If you ask the question, they answer the way you want them to, then the answer is both of yours, and you all have ownership over that answer.

Most coaches have the default setting: Tell versus ask. Asking produces a two-way discussion that increases ownership. That was an effective tool that Mike used to help change the culture of USA Basketball when he was named National Team coach.

When Mike took over the Olympic team in 2008, the National Team was coming off its worst finish in history. The team went 5–3 and finished third.

I asked Mike, "What was the most important team-building exercise you did with that squad?"

Mike Krzyzewski
Duke

Probably the most important one I've had was the night before we started practice with the Olympic team, the 2008 gold medal team in Beijing, where we never talked about basketball. We talked about standards.

These are things that Kobe Bryant, Jason Kidd, LeBron James, Dwyane Wade, and all these guys said. It was about how we were going to live. And everybody on the team contributed. And we came up with a list of standards.

Not being late, no excuses, being flexible, looking each other in the eye, always telling each other the truth, having each other's back. And when we left the room, they became the way we were going to live together. And it was a great team-building exercise.

What did Mike not talk about? Basketball. Instead, the team established the standards of how they were going to live with one another. Take a look at this list:

TEAM USA
STANDARDS
WHO WE ARE

DON'T BE LATE	NO EXCUSES
BE FLEXIBLE	LOOK EACH OTHER IN THE EYE
ALWAYS TELL THE TRUTH	HAVE EACH OTHER'S BACK

If you compare that to the kindergarten list, it's a very similar process.

When Mike asked each member of the team to bring a standard, what did that do? It created ownership, which ultimately created team accountability. That process is not dictated; it's collaborative.

Another nuance, and this may seem like semantics: What's the difference between a "standard" and a "rule"?

The purpose of a standard is to motivate and inspire. The purpose of a rule is to enforce control.

Think about the different energy between standards and rules. One is about choosing to be your best. The other is about following a requirement imposed on you by an outside force—where there is no choice.

From a management position, standards also give you more latitude to deal with the gray area of each situation. Rules are black and white and can back you into a corner. All of these things affirm Mike Krzyzewski's approach with the Olympic team, and if you were to ask him what the primary responsibility of a coach is, here's what he would say:

Mike Krzyzewski
Duke

Your primary responsibility as a coach is to become one with the player and then become one with the team. And that's what you should be spending most of your time on.

It's such a powerful answer, but also easy to miss. The job is to become one.

Think about this. If you gave your team a word off the following list (next page) and asked them to write down their definition, how many different answers would you get?

PERFORMANCE SKILLS	**RELATIONAL SKILLS**
Hardworking: Paying the price with effort	**Unselfish:** Putting the team first
Competitive: Striving to be your best	**Honest:** Telling the truth
Positive: Good and useful thinking	**Respectful:** Showing consideration
Focused: Eliminating distractions	**Appreciative:** Recognizing the good in someone or something
Accountable: Taking responsibility for your actions	**Humble:** Distributing credit
Courageous: Operating outside of your comfort zone	**Patient:** Tolerating delay or struggle
Resilient: Bouncing back from setbacks	**Loyal:** Showing allegiance
Confident: Self-trusting	**Trustworthy:** Being reliable
Enthusiastic: Expressing enjoyment	**Trustwilling:** Relying on others
Disciplined: Self-regulating	**Encouraging:** Giving confidence and support
Motivated: Having a strong purpose	**Socially Aware:** Understanding signals sent and received
Creative: Out-of-the-box thinking	**Caring:** Investing in the person
Curious: Desiring to learn or understand	**Empathetic:** Sharing the feelings of others

Becoming one is getting on the same page. It's closing the gap of interpretation. It's defining these characteristics in a simple way that everyone understands, and bringing them to life so it becomes part of your team's identity.

I worked with softball coach Missy Lombardi on her transition from being a four-time National Champion assistant coach to being a first-time head coach at the University of Oregon. The previous coach at Oregon had success, but approached coaching in a completely different way than Missy did.

It was a hard transition. Missy's way was much different than what the team was used to.

Missy worked to redefine the program through "Duck ID" sessions.

DUCK ID

Each session she would bring information that helped define who they were becoming, how they did things, and why they were doing it.

WHAT DRIVES WINNING ENVIRONMENTS 33

In two years, she went from being unsure if they were even going to be able to field a roster (because of a high number of transfers) to being in the top ten.

How does this relate to you? And as a coach, where do you start? Let's look at a road map for how to approach defining your expectations with your team.

DEFINE ROAD MAP

 WHAT'S THE CURRICULUM AT YOUR HOW U?

Start with this thought: Anything that is expected should be defined. Ask yourself, "What do I expect?" (That can be overwhelming!)

Here's how I helped start How U with a basketball team that I worked with. I sat behind the bench and watched one game. I wrote down everything that wasn't functioning up to the standard that they were trying to achieve. Here's the list I came up with from that game:

HOW U

Move a teammate to the next play	Coach from the bench
Get subbed out after a bad call	Handle a bad call
Engage from the bench (demeanor)	Move past miscommunication
Receive instruction (coaching)	Echo communication
Huddle	Handle an opponent trash talking
Have next-play speed	Self-regulate in hostile environments
Help a teammate up after a hustle play	Move past success
Participate in a film session	Handle disappointment with decisions
Warm up before the second half	Get past a defensive breakdown

I showed this to the head coach the next day. His response, "We can't even break a press." We laughed.

I asked him, "Have you formally taught what each of these look like when executed successfully?" He looked like he had just seen a ghost.

None of these things have anything to do with the Xs and Os of basketball. But they have everything to do with winning. The teams that can do these things when it counts the most give themselves the best chance at winning. Why wouldn't you teach them?

Defining can range from broad (the identity of our team) to specific (how to clean your space) topics.

What's one thing you need to better define for your team?

DEFINE		

 HOW DO YOU TEACH IT IN A CREATIVE WAY?

Chris Petersen, former Washington football coach, created a staff development tool called 5-Star Coaching. One component of 5-Star Coaching was to become a master teacher.

Chris defined a master teacher as *someone who inspires learning.* He came to realize the importance of that when he became a first-time head coach. Chris started to attend the meetings run by his assistant coaches, and he noticed the different levels of his coaches' teaching abilities:

THE COACHES' TEACHING ABILITIES

Coach 1 ▮
Coach 2 ▮▮▮▮▮▮
Coach 3 ▮▮▮
Coach 4 ▮▮▮▮▮▮▮
Coach 5 ▮▮▮▮▮

Coach 6 ▮
Coach 7 ▮▮▮▮▮▮▮▮
Coach 8 ▮▮▮▮▮▮▮▮▮▮
Coach 9 ▮▮▮▮▮▮▮▮

His eyes were opened. He started to project into the future, and he realized how much further along Coach #4's group would be compared to Coach #1's. Guess what they did? They unpacked and defined what a good teacher looks like and what a good meeting looks like. Here's an example of how Chris would inspire learning with his team:

Chris Petersen
Washington

If I would come at our guys and give them rules on what not to do on a Saturday night, it would go in one ear and out the other. So you have to find a creative way to grab their attention and have a discussion.

I set up a skit. I grabbed a freshman that didn't really know what was going on and I said, "We're going to role play a Saturday night and you're at a bar where you shouldn't be. Just play along with me."

So we have this bar setup in the front of the room with two cups of beer in it.

I come walking in, our team is watching, there's 130 people in the room, and I come up next to him and say, "What's your name?" He says his name. I ask, "What do you do here?" He says, "I play football."

I start giving him the business. "They suck. Your coach sucks." Then I take the beer and throw it in his face. He's shocked. The team erupts. You can see the fire in his eyes. And I hold my fist up like we're going to fight.

It's a great way to create energy and unpack that as a team, because that situation has and will happen.

What's Chris done? He's created context in an experiential way. He doesn't want his players to experience those moments for the first time without having the social agility to deal with them.

What you cover on the front end reflects your experience.

Chris covers the bar scene along with what happens when your teammate gets cornered by a group, or a guy hits on your girlfriend. Why? He's seen it before, so he wants to get ahead of these issues by defining what it looks like to be able to navigate those moments.

Talking about it isn't enough. Master teachers inspire learning through creativity.

How could you teach in a creative way?
↓

DEFINE	TEACH	

HOW DO YOU MEASURE UNDERSTANDING?

Chris Petersen craves feedback. He has a staff retreat each year to get everybody on the same page. One year he decided he wanted to measure how well the staff understood the messages from the retreat, and ultimately measure his effectiveness as a teacher:

Chris Petersen
Washington

Every year we go away somewhere cool for a staff retreat to lock in to the way we're going to do things. We've been with each other for years, so you assume that they got it. We have a great retreat and we come back and I'm on the plane and I'm thinking, "Did they really get it?" I don't know why it hit me right then.

So I walk in the next day, "Hey guys, I want to give you a test on what I covered at the retreat." You should have seen the look on their faces. It was like the blood drained out. They were like, "What?!"

I reassured them that this was for me. I wasn't testing them. I was testing myself on how well I communicated the message. And I was shocked when I got the test back. We assume, because it's our world, that everybody gets it. It was an eye-opening way for me to measure understanding.

To reinforce what Chris said, that test was for him as a teacher, not to grade his coaches. I ask coaches how they measure understanding with their team. Here are some of their answers:

Ask questions: If you cold-call, it gives you control on whose voice you want to hear.

Have athletes write down their thoughts: It's an efficient way to gather everyone's thoughts and have them engage deeper with what you're teaching. When you read and ask them about what they wrote down, it signals that you're listening.

Organize small group discussions: When you divide your team into small groups, you can have them explore the content together and then ask each group what they took away from it.

Pay attention: If it's not functioning properly, that's feedback that you need to become better at Defining.

Now look back at your example:

How could you measure understanding?

DEFINE	TEACH	MEASURE

ROAD MAP REVIEW

WHAT'S THE CURRICULUM AT YOUR HOW U?

HOW DO YOU TEACH IT IN A CREATIVE WAY?

HOW DO YOU MEASURE UNDERSTANDING?

MANAGE

Author's Note

Any time you define a clear expectation you are drawing a line between what's acceptable and what's unacceptable.

Anson Dorrance, head women's soccer coach at the University of North Carolina, had a great line about managing. He said, "Players do what you inspect, not what you expect."

Coaches spend a lot of time managing behavior. Urban Meyer, former Ohio State football coach, wrote a book called *Above The Line*.

The idea is that anything that met or exceeded the standard of their program was considered above-the-line behavior. Anything that didn't was considered below-the-line behavior.

There are two components that I'm going to explore with you in the Manage section:

- One: How to catch above-the-line behavior.
- Two: How to convert below-the-line behavior.

We'll start with catching above-the-line behavior.

MANAGE
CATCHING ABOVE-THE-LINE BEHAVIOR

CATCHING ABOVE-THE-LINE BEHAVIOR

What do you think about this quote?

Mike Krzyzewski
Duke

We as coaches can always catch a kid doing something wrong and we overlook the things that they're doing right. They'll do less wrong things if we catch the right things.

Do you agree? They'll do less wrong things if we catch the right things. Is that true for your players?

We had a panel at our 2016 What Drives Winning conference where we discussed this thought and Jack Clark, head coach of Cal rugby, weighed in:

Jack Clark
Cal-Berkeley

Well just keeping it real as a coach, I probably got that wrong for about twenty years. I'm from the McAfee clan and there's always something wrong, and I was the guy that always pointed it out.

Brett: *Why do you think it took you so long?*

Well, we were successful. And, it's hard to audit success. It takes a bit of experience to really make changes when you're winning. But it's the right thing to do.

If we were having a bad training session I called the team in and just gave them the business because somebody had a physical breakdown, a skill breakdown, a mental breakdown, and they're box-carring those mistakes together. I really had twenty years of giving them the business and sending them back out there, and it never got better once.

Then you find a way to, as Coach K says, find something positive. Guy passes the ball to another guy, it's a good pass, the guy drops it. It drives me crazy the guy dropped the ball, but I say, "Good pass." And with just some positive speak sometimes you can really pull a team out of a funk.

You got to keep it real. I mean, you can't say, "You look sharp in your unis today."

I think there's a way with positive speak to build the right culture and at the same time pull a team out of a funk.

This is not the default setting for coaches. For experienced coaches with high standards, it's easy to fall into the trap of catching and pointing out what needs to be fixed. Geno Auriemma, UConn women's basketball coach, unpacked that:

Geno Auriemma
Connecticut

There are a lot of coaches, me included, that are hoarders. We hoard every play.

So if a kid makes a mistake, five minutes later, after they've had five great minutes of basketball and they make a mistake that's similar to the one they made five minutes ago, you can't wait to pile on that same mistake and revisit that history.

So I think as coaches, if we are the kind of coaches that let go of what just happened and focus on "make the next play," I think your players start to play like that. Now, some struggle with that.

Don't get me wrong. But I think we as coaches can really be influential in that area. And I found that when I'm a hoarder and like waiting to pile it on, they're waiting to make the next mistake.

When I let it go and I just say, "Come on, let's go, move on to the next thing," they move on to the next thing.

So many coaches relate to the idea of hoarding, including Kelly Inouye-Perez, UCLA's softball coach. She reflected on her biggest regret the first year she was a head coach:

Kelly Inouye-Perez
UCLA

A lot of people ask me, "What's your worst moment as a coach?" I remember my low. It was my first year as a head coach. I was in the dugout and we were not playing well. I was writing everything down that we were doing wrong.

We should have done this! We should have done that! My list got to double-digits of all these things that were wrong. It was almost like I was anticipating and looking for all the failures.

Then we had our postgame meeting, and of course, because I'm such a smart coach, I let them have it with the tone of what I was feeling when I was writing everything down. So I said everything, "We did this. And we did that!"

And I remember looking up and I will never forget the look on all of their faces. I completely sold out on them and was what I now see was Captain Obvious.

Think about what Kelly just said. Compare that with what Mike Krzyzewski said: "They'll do less wrong things if you catch the right things." It's unnatural for a lot of coaches to catch the right things. That's why we need to train ourselves.

Mike is going to break down what he considers a *right thing*:

Mike Krzyzewski
Duke

A right thing is not just hitting a bucket. A right thing is a kid saying something that is encouraging.

A right thing is a block out, a rebound, being smart in a certain situation, being enthusiastic on the bench, helping a teammate.

Point those things out. Point out winning plays because you want them to do it over and over again.

Winning plays are things that often go unnoticed to the untrained eye, but that contribute to winning. What are some of the winning plays you need to catch as a coach?

Think back to the How U list I made for the basketball team that we covered in the Define section. (See the following page.) These have nothing to do with Xs and Os, but they have everything to do with winning. The irony is, for coaches, it's easy to get distracted by the Xs and Os to the point that you don't recognize any of these things when they happen.

HOW U

Move a teammate to the next play	Coach from the bench
Get subbed out after a bad call	Handle a bad call
Engage from the bench (demeanor)	Move past miscommunication
Receive instruction (coaching)	Echo communication
Huddle	Handle an opponent trash talking
Have next-play speed	Self-regulate in hostile environments
Help a teammate up after a hustle play	Move past success
Participate in a film session	Handle disappointment with decisions
Warm up before the second half	Get past a defensive breakdown

You have to retrain the lens through which you watch the game. I learned this lesson when I worked with coaches outside of basketball. I didn't understand the nuances of the game they were coaching.

The only things I could see were on the human level and how coaches and players responded to the events of the game. My attention was freed up and unshackled from the details of physical execution, so I could see what was happening outside of the sport-specific action.

I do a lot of work with college coaches, which is the last stop for athletes before they enter the real world. If the athlete's environment is one of high expectations where they're constantly told, "not good enough," it can be easy to internalize that. There can be residual effects on how they view themselves when they leave college having been immersed in a culture of perfectionism.

I put together a playbook to get you thinking about how to catch above-the-line behavior as your team chases the high standards of your program.

ABOVE-THE-LINE PLAYBOOK

PRAISE THE MODEL

P.J. Fleck
Minnesota

We talk about "Praising the Model." With everything that we're teaching, there is someone who's going to do it correctly. We use that player to highlight exactly what we want. We don't teach them what we don't want. We want to teach them what we do want.

Coaches know that you can't cover everything before you start. When you praise the model in the present moment, that's a way for you to educate everyone in the environment on what your program standard is.

I asked Bill Belichick, "What's the most important thing your veterans do to orient your newcomers into the environment?"

He responded, "The most important thing a vet can do is do his job."

If we combine what Bill says with what P.J. says, it's clear. When the veteran does his job, what's he doing? He's providing an example of how to do something. In P.J.'s environment, he's going to highlight that as a way to teach everybody else the standard.

One of the things that separates coaches is what they are able to see.

For example, here's a player who is making an aggressive play toward the basket:

The ref calls an offensive foul. This player has been working on what we call "Next-Play Speed." In fact, it's written on the sole of his shoe as a reminder. He's training himself to get to the next play and not get stuck in the past.

He executes that perfectly in this clip. He sets the ball down and runs back on defense instantly:

If you're looking at this from a basketball-only perspective, being called for a charge isn't a desired outcome. But if you train your lens to see the player's response instead, you're now coaching what influences winning more than a single play.

What do you do when things don't go your way? That's what this player is working on, and the only way for him to get better at that skill is to experience things that don't go his way. If we don't praise that as coaches, we miss an opportunity to create real growth and development.

BUILD AN IDENTITY

This bulldog logo is powerful:

It symbolizes decades of excellence. What's cool about Gonzaga, though, is that despite all the experience and understanding of what excellence should look like from a coach's perspective, they still foster a bottom-up approach.

Strength coach Travis Knight drives that. That's why this thumbprint behind the bulldog is important.

It speaks to the process of growth. It allows the team to grow into their own identity.

A phrase that really resonated with the 2020 team was this: What is real is unspoken.

Here's how they used that statement to reinforce the actions that reflected Gonzaga's values. In basketball, it's common to have highlight reels. Gonzaga made a different reel. They called it a "Highlight Real."

What made the Real? Actions that reflected who they were at their best. After Travis would show them the clips that communicated that, the thumbprint would animate in as visual imagery of what was happening.

WHAT DRIVES WINNING ENVIRONMENTS   53

At the end of the year, right before the tournament, Travis flashed this on the screen:

LOADING THE REAL

When the progress bar filled in, it cut to all of the clips that had been compiled from the year to show the identity that this team had created for themselves. Being yourself under pressure is one of the hardest things to do. That's why Travis spends so much time cultivating an identity that grows from the bottom up. It reminds them of who they are.

Gonzaga didn't just use clips to highlight Real. They also used statements that were made throughout the season. For example, in January Gonzaga was ranked number one in the country and they dominated their opponents. The next week, when rankings came out, despite Gonzaga winning, experts picked Baylor ahead of them.

Travis asked the team how they felt about that. The starting guard said this:

> "I didn't care when they ranked us one. Why would I care if they ranked us two?"

He understands that rankings are opinions, and that as a team they build their own reality. Take a look at the bottom right of that graphic. Do you see the thumbprint? That's an ID Statement. It's another way to highlight (especially for coaches who don't have access to video) the identity of the team.

When you associate actions and statements with imagery (like the thumbprint) that links to an identity, it becomes a powerful reinforcement tool.

Another example of a program doing this is Oklahoma football. This image means a lot to them, **OU**DNA: →

In the 2019–20 season, they had a leader at the quarterback position: Jalen Hurts. Jalen transferred from Alabama.

He put his stamp on the team. Here's an example of that: →

This is after a game that they won. Is he improving his fitness? Maybe. What's he really doing? He's demonstrating his mentality to the team.

When your leader does that, you can attach the action with a symbol to communicate who you are.

Back to what Bill Belichick said, "The most important thing a vet can do is do his job." That's what Jalen Hurts is doing. Great coaches spotlight that.

ORCHESTRATE PEER RECOGNITION

Here's how Mike Krzyzewski introduces this concept to his team:

Mike Krzyzewski
Duke

First of all, I'd sit down with them individually and tell them that they have the talent to do that. I think sometimes we say, "Well, this kid could do it," but we never tell him that he can do it or how to do it.

You give him suggestions like, "It'd be really good if you pat someone on the back. Today, I'd like for you, if Jimmy is down or after he misses his first shot, to go up to him and say, 'Keep shooting,'" and so you give him different things like that.

What a coach says is important. But what a peer says to another is so darn important, especially if that guy who's the best player says something to another player. It's such a force multiplier on a team. And it produces a connection because it's all based on care. "I care enough about you to help you in that regard."

For young athletes, it's easy for them to get fixated on their own performance. When you're focused on that, it's easy to miss what's around you. For most, they haven't come to understand the power of their influence because they haven't experienced positive reinforcement from it.

That's why so many coaches love this idea from Kelly Inouye-Perez. Kelly would think about what her team needed based on where they were in the year. She would then present a word of the day. The team and coaches worked on defining it together and once they did, here's what they would do:

Kelly Inouye-Perez
UCLA

Your words become more powerful when you get your players to talk about not just the word, or concept, but examples of it. Whatever word I say, I ask what that looks like and then I ask for examples and have them shout it out. We circle up a lot and have our players talk about it. Otherwise, they just become words.

Kelly is facilitating peer shout-outs. What Kelly has come to understand with this process is that her players catch far more than she does as a coach.

By having the shout-outs, it brings to light things that would otherwise never get brought up and increases the functionality of the team.

ENCOURAGING BEHAVIORAL STREAKS

In 2018, Geno Auriemma made this statement at the What Drives Winning conference in Chicago:

Geno Auriemma
Connecticut

I've had kids come to me and say, "Coach, I want to win a national championship. I want be an All-American. I want to play on the Olympic team. I want to play pro."

I had one kid in her sophomore year, I called her into the office and I said, "Remember what you told me?" And she said, "Yeah."

I said, "Well it's not going to happen. Watching you for two years here, it's not going to happen. So here are your choices: Change your goals or change your work habits."

One of the questions I like to ask players after they hear that is this: What's an unproductive habit that you need to say goodbye to? Or what's a productive habit you want to commit to?

Whatever they identify, the goal then becomes to build a streak, to stack days. How many days can you stack? That activates their competitive mode in order to change habits that don't align with their goals.

The question is: How do you get them addicted to the standard? In other words, how do you get them to want to do the work? Streaks are a great way to highlight productive behavior to create the consistency necessary in pursuit of their goals.

EXPRESS APPRECIATION

Anson Dorrance, head women's soccer coach at the University of North Carolina, has a higher winning percentage in National Championship games than he does all other games. Think about that. In games that are the hardest to win, they're at their best. Here's what he does the day before that game:

Anson Dorrance
North Carolina

If a team gets to the National Championship game, I spend the entire day in preparation for this championship moment by writing a letter to every senior on my roster thanking her for the incredible human contribution she's made to my team.

He's won 22 out of 24 national championships. Anson says that the letters are what drives the percentage:

Anson Dorrance
North Carolina

It's the fuel, that against the best team in the country, on the final day of the season that puts us in a position that out of 24 games we won 22. Here's an even extended impact of these letters.

One year, I was in a panic, we're in the Final Four and I'm looking at our bracket and I'm thinking, "You know what? I think I have to use the senior letter in the semifinal." The team we were playing in the semifinal was Portland. They were absolutely unbelievable.

Sure enough, I'm carving away at these letters. I'm handing them out, and yep, my team delivers me to the finals, where we promptly lost by the way. So the letters have actually worked 23 out of 24 times.

What's going on with those letters? What does that speak to? It speaks to the power of genuine appreciation.

In a high-performing environment, it's very easy to take talent for granted, and when that happens, it's a completely different atmosphere.

Geno Auriemma shares the experience he had after winning his first National Championship and what's happened since:

Geno Auriemma
Connecticut

It was like a concert when we walked into the arena. And it hasn't happened since. So they don't really give a crap anymore. Now it's like, "What the hell? You're causing traffic." They couldn't care less now.

Geno has won 11 National Championships. They haven't celebrated any like they did the first one. Think about that. How unfair is it to the players who have just won their first championship?

Here's something to consider: Expectations without appreciation leads to a cold, entitled environment.

What does that sound like?

- "You did what you're supposed to do. Why would I praise that?"
- "Silence is praise. You'll hear me when you're wrong."
- "On to the next."

As a coach, how would you feel if your administration approached you with this mentality? It's so easy to fall into that trap. That's why NBA coach Billy Donovan says this:

Billy Donovan
Chicago Bulls

When you accomplish something really, really good, I always felt like there should be a great celebration. Always.

60 BRETT LEDBETTER

Because the minute you start creating a level of expectation or "this is supposed to happen," I think you create an environment of entitlement and you lose perspective of how hard it actually is.

If you don't appreciate your people for their contribution, think about how that would feel and what kind of effect it would have.

One important nuance to point out: There's a difference between expressing appreciation and praising the model. Praising the model is a strategy used to educate everybody in the environment on what the standard is. Expressing appreciation is for the individual. It's personal. It's heartfelt. It's a way to show that you are truly grateful for their contribution. And that's powerful.

PLAYBOOK REVIEW

PRAISE THE MODEL

BUILD AN IDENTITY

ORCHESTRATE PEER RECOGNITION

ENCOURAGE BEHAVIORAL STREAKS

EXPRESS APPRECIATION

MANAGE
CONVERTING BELOW-THE-LINE BEHAVIOR

CONVERTING BELOW-THE-LINE BEHAVIOR

We've just explored how to catch above-the-line behavior; now we're going to look at how to convert below-the-line behavior. To start, here's a thought from Tim Corbin, head baseball coach at Vanderbilt:

Tim Corbin
Vanderbilt

What you allow will come back either positively or negatively. And I just think the allowance of behaviors, good or bad, is really the setting of what's going to come forward.

Let's look at a concrete example. After scoring a touchdown, a player made the throat-slash gesture. It's not an uncommon gesture in sports, but it cost the team a 15-yard penalty:

Here's how the coach handled it:

He blew up at the player on the sidelines in front of all his peers. You can see everybody observing this interaction in the picture. When I ask coaches what the pros and cons of this approach are, what do you think they say?

Biggest Pro: It's efficient. You are clearly communicating the standards in a memorable way for everybody on the team to see.

Biggest Con: It's hard to ask your players for poise if you aren't displaying it as a coach.

Question for you: How you would define the word "agility"?

One coach answered that question, "To be able to change directions quickly and smoothly." Now if we apply his answer to the social context, it means having the ability to change directions quickly and smoothly when situations catch you off guard. That's a required skill for reaching competitive maturity.

What's competitive maturity? To be able to be your best, authentic self in highly competitive environments. That's hard to do. But how you navigate situations that catch you off guard is where credibility is earned and lost with your team.

Here's an example of that. Earl Thomas, one of the best players on the Seattle Seahawks, tore his ACL in the fourth game of the year. It was a contract year. As he was being carted off the field, this was the gesture he made at head coach Pete Carroll:

Pete Carroll was asked about this in the postgame press conference. Here's how he responded:

Pete Carroll
Seattle Seahawks

Under the circumstances to handle what just happened, in a flash of a moment, with all of the knowledge . . . he knows exactly what the injury [is]. I'm sure it flashed in his mind, "It's going to take this long this time." You know, all of the stuff that's going through his head.

I mean you got to give anybody a break, you know. You can have expectations for people to do exactly as you would think they should do. But until you're there doing it, you can't understand it. And so that's exactly how I feel about it. I know that probably some of the other players, people who have been in the situation, understand.

I get it when people want to pass judgment and try to cast aspersions about something. But in the heat of the moment, with all the emotional part of this, and the injury and the pain and all of that. . . Shoot man, give the guy a break.

High-level coaches will say, "That's the gold standard." Pete killed the story before the reporter could even print it. It takes an incredible amount of wisdom and compassion to operate from that place. That's a professional approach.

It's an approach that's opposite of what most coaches use. Most use what we call Power Tools, which we define as "strategies to force control."

What are some of the most common Power Tools coaches use? Limiting playing time, running sprints, and public humiliation are all examples of exercising your authority. If you rely on power, you put a ceiling on your development and upward mobility as a coach. There will be scenarios that require a more sophisticated approach if you want to coach high-level talent. Let's look at how Power Tools can backfire.

Jay Williams played college basketball at Duke for Mike Krzyzewski. Then he was drafted by the Chicago Bulls, and this is what he observed his rookie year:

Jay Williams
Former NBA Player

Think about the culture I came from at Duke. You're there early. You're there late. You dress for the job you want, not for the job you have. A first-class culture.

Then you get to the league and your GM at the time, Jerry Krause, says, "Hey, look, guys, we need to start approaching this game differently. We want everybody to wear a suit and tie on the bus before every game, mandatory. If not, you're going to get fined $15,000." So as a 21-year-old kid, that's a lot of money.

Then the first day after he says that, you see your leader, your team captain, Jalen Rose, show up in a camouflage jumpsuit. And you're like, "Oh, okay, this is a rebellious team-like mentality." And he does it every day. You start calculating. That's $15K. That's $30K. That's $45K. That's $60K. And it doesn't faze him. It's a trickle-down effect.

When you force someone into doing something, that's extrinsic motivation. They're doing it because they have to, not because they want to. That can turn into a volatile situation.

That's why Boston Celtics coach Brad Stevens takes a different approach. I asked him, "What's your philosophy on punishment?"

Brad Stevens
Boston Celtics

I'm not a big punishment person. We don't run sprints. We don't do any of that stuff. We just want intrinsically motivated guys who are trying to be the best they can be.

He's operating with a different set of tools. He's a pro. And if we were going to define what Pro Tools are, we would simply say, "strategies to win influence." Using logic, listening and meeting people where they are would be examples of Pro Tools.

If we contrast Power Tools with Pro Tools:

POWER TOOLS
Force Control

VS

PRO TOOLS
Win Influence

Those two methods create totally different kinds of energy. It's important to note that Pro Tools have nothing to do with the level at which you compete. It has everything to do with your approach. Pro Tools can be implemented at any level—from youth leagues to professional organizations. Let's explore a playbook on how you can win influence and convert below-the-line behavior.

Author's Note

One of my favorite questions to ask coaches is, "When do you know when to force control versus win influence?"

Chris Petersen had a great answer. He said, "Our saying is 'win 'em over' or 'weed 'em out.'"

The beauty of this thought is how universal it is. It can be as big or small as you need it to be. You can weed someone out of a drill, a practice, a game, a season, or the program, depending on the context.

We all know there has to be an enforcement mechanism. One of the hardest questions coaches face is, "When do you know when to cut someone loose?" There comes a point when you realize that you can't save everyone. But you can fight like hell to win influence, and up next are some strategies to help you get there.

BELOW-THE-LINE PLAYBOOK

➡ COACH THE NEXT-PLAY MENTALITY

This is a strategy to use in the moment. Brad Stevens says, "Basketball is an emotional game of random events." Anytime you're dealing with random events, you will make mistakes. High-level coaches understand that:

Mike Krzyzewski
Duke

The game is a game of mistakes. You're going to make mistakes in this game. It's too fast. No one's perfect, but you can't let a mistake lead to another mistake.

How do you not let mistakes compound? Here's an exercise that I did with a team I worked with. I asked, "What are the events that pull you from the present moment?" Here's the list that they came up with:

EVENTS

Turnover	Teammate makes a bad pass
Being subbed out	Coach calling you out
Obnoxious fan	Selfish teammate
Missing a shot	Parent distractions
Bad call	Mixed signals from coaches
Playing time	Opponents talking trash

What do you notice when you read this list? If you did this with your team, what would they say?

After we created the list, I showed the team a video clip of Mike Krzyzewski describing why it's important to have a next-play mentality:

Mike Krzyzewski
Duke

You cannot do anything for the last play. In other words, someone who is always looking in his rearview mirror will never make the most of the current moment. And so the next play is the next moment. So why wouldn't you want to be at your best for the next moment?

The team and I built from this concept. We came up with the term "Next-Play Speed." We talked about how fast they could move past the last play, whether it was good or bad. This team needed an added layer of accountability, so I shared an idea with the head coach.

There was a student manager on the team that all of the guys respected. I asked the coach, "What if we made his role the NPC? The Next-Play Coach. His one job: move people to the next play."

The coach was supportive. I ran the idea by the student manager; he was excited. In three weeks, he went from wearing khakis and a polo to wearing a uniform on the bench (and eventually getting a scholarship), because he had that strong of an impact on the team.

There are moments when there's no time to teach, and in those instances this is a great strategy to keep things moving. When there's a break, you can assess if the behavior is a one-off that doesn't need to be addressed, or if it's part of a developing pattern. If it's a developing pattern, that can lead us into the next strategy.

FACILITATE SELF-COACHING

A coach approached me and said, "We have a really good shooter. But he's getting in his own way and it's affecting his performance. Can you talk to him?"

This player has a chance to be the best shooter in the history of this prestigious school. I wanted to start off the conversation positioning myself as the student. One of my favorite lines in coaching comes from Jack Clark. He said, "Why guess when you can know?"

I knew he hadn't forgotten how to shoot. I wanted to know what he thought about his own situation, so I asked him, "How would you coach a teammate that's going through the exact same situation that you're going through?"

I asked him to take five minutes to write down his thoughts, which would create an added layer of ownership that we could return to in the future. Here's what he wrote down:

You need to quit overthinking things.

Start selectively listening to your circle. They're making you second guess everything the coaches say.

You know that you don't just bring value when you score, you do a lot of things to impact the game. When you listen to them, it feels like the only way you add value is if you score.

This team needs you to be much more than a scorer. This team needs you to be a leader. When you're thinking about you, you're not thinking about the team and they see that.

After reading that, what do you think?

In my experience, this happens often. When you give athletes the space and help reframe their situation so they can see it clearly without judgment, it's amazing to hear how they would approach it from a coaching standpoint.

It's also amazing to think that a lot of coaches look at this from a basketball-only perspective and say, "Look, man, you just need to get extra shots up." There's more to what's happening than meets the eye.

The reality is this player can coach himself much better than I ever could. After we unlocked what's inside of him, my challenge to him was this: If you won't listen to you, why would anyone else?

That seemed to really resonate with him, because he wants to be a strong leader for his team. From there, my work became supporting and challenging him to take his own advice. That's how I attacked it on an individual level. Here's how I would do it on a collective level.

I would compile film of examples when the team isn't performing up to their standard. For example, there was a miscommunication with a team I was working with. The point guard threw the ball at the same time that his teammate cut to the basket and the ball went out of bounds. Turnover. I asked the team, "How would a championship team handle this event?"

They said, "Own it. Move past it together."

I then showed how they actually handled it (which didn't line up with their answer). They nodded their heads. From there, we moved on. I'm not injecting my opinions into the team. I'm facilitating a discussion where they can communicate how they're going to manage the situation in the future if it comes up again.

ALIGN SELF-INTEREST

Think about the people you lead. What percentage of their thoughts is anchored in self-interest versus in the greater good? When I ask coaches that question, they smile. The majority of people they lead think and act out of self-interest. That's why this strategy can be effective.

What I've come to realize is that self-interest is often stronger than loyalty, and I think great coaches understand that. Tom Izzo, who coaches basketball at Michigan State, said this was the biggest mistake he made as a young coach:

Tom Izzo
Michigan State

I wanted everything because it was right for me and I didn't spend enough time trying to understand what they wanted. And that changed really quick. I started to get a better feel, through more team meetings, for what they want and have them explain it. So I'm doing it with them. I'm not doing it for me.

I think when you get in college, especially where you're hired and fired based on wins and losses, you want to win, win, win, win, win. But if you've got a kid who just wants to play or just wants to be better or maybe just wants to be a pro, and doesn't want to win, you better figure that out quick. And figure out how to align your goals, because as Jud Heathcote used to say, "Every good deal is a good deal for both parties."

WHAT DRIVES WINNING ENVIRONMENTS   75

Here's what that looks like in action. I was working with a basketball team that had a very talented freshman. The draft boards had him projected as a top-ten draft pick. He was having a tough time transitioning into the environment. The coach asked if I could help.

Here's what I handed him: →

This looks like the NBA draft board. I gave everyone on the team a copy.

On the top of the page I asked everybody to put their name next to GM (General Manager). Then I asked, "How would you pick this team, in order, if the objective was to win open gym today?"

Everyone (including the staff) wrote down how they would pick the team. We then took the answers and created a composite score and a self-score. The results were surprising.

Remember, the athlete I was working with was a top-ten draft pick according to mock drafts. His teammates picked him sixth—that's outside the starting five. He picked himself seventh. Going into this exercise, where do you think I thought he would pick himself? First, right? Which goes back to Jack Clark's line, "Why guess when you can know?"

I brought him in individually and shared the data with him. I praised his self-awareness and I asked him, "What would you want an NBA scout to tell the GM after watching you play this year?" He wrote down his answer:

76   BRETT LEDBETTER

He loves the game and can fit into a high-level organization while his skill and experience catch up. He's an elite defender, teammate, and is coachable. All of those things are shown through his responses.

My work with this player became to build a curriculum for him to help this become a reality. Do you see how that aligns his self-interest with the team's interests? He wants to go to the NBA. If he does all of those things (that he wants a scout to see), do you see how that will help his current team?

I love aligning self-interest with team goals because it's fair. As coaches, you're negotiating for your athlete's best energy every day. That's a big ask. It's important that the athlete feels like they're getting something valuable out of the experience.

It's important to note that the only way you can align self-interest is to know what that person wants, which comes from truly understanding your players.

DEVELOP MIDDLE-LAYER MANAGEMENT

I asked Kelly Graves, head coach of the Oregon women's basketball team, "What's the best way to change undesired behavior?" Here's what he said:

Kelly Graves
Oregon

I would first talk to the senior leadership and say, "Hey, I don't want to make a big deal of this, but we've got to get this person in line. We need her. And if we let this behavior go, then we're going to have issues."

Why is this effective? Kelly doesn't have to burn any bullets as a leader fixing that issue.

He gets to observe and coach the leadership of his team as opposed to micromanaging the problem. That gives the head coach a strong sense of how effective his or her leaders are.

University of Oklahoma's softball coach, Patty Gasso, has a lot of examples of what strong female leadership looks like. Her program has produced some incredible leaders.

This past year, I met with their leadership group and they said that they were having a difficult time getting the underclassmen to live up to the team standards on and off the field. They asked me for some advice on how to reach the underclassmen.

I challenged them. I asked, "If your teammates were going to rank you in these four categories on a scale of 1–10, how would they rank you?"

How much do they feel:
___ Listened to
___ Needed
___ Cared for
___ Appreciated

There was a long pause. It felt like they had never thought about those things before. I shared a story with them. Brad Stevens was once asked, "How do you change undesired behavior of someone on your team whose standard is below the line?"

He said, "I rebound for them."

Think about how powerful that is. When you invest sweat equity by serving your teammates, you build trust and begin to understand what's driving their behavior. From there, you can figure out how to influence them. The seniors loved that story and reframed their approach with the underclassmen (and made remarkable strides).

RETEACH

A teacher asked their class to alphabetize these words:

water
green
craft
steak
apple

Here's how one of the students responded:

aertw
eegnr
acfrt
aekst
aelpp

What does that show us? Everyone interprets things differently, and that's why P.J. Fleck says one of the best lessons he learned teaching fifth graders was how to teach the same thing a hundred different ways. Former football coach Chris Petersen has a great story about that:

Chris Petersen
Washington

I was a young wide-receiver coach. One of my responsibilities was to teach them how to align correctly; if you don't, you're going to get a penalty. It's day-one type stuff.

So we're in game four, and sure enough, the same guy that I can't really reach on this basic stuff gets another penalty. And my coach, who was a mentor, walks up to me. I quickly say to him, "This is the dumbest guy I've coached."

The head coach says, "I could teach my yellow lab how to get on and off the ball. This is on you, not on him. Teach him a different way." And after thirty years, that has stuck with me.

Chris adopted a new mentality: There are no bad students, only poor teaching. That's how he approaches it. If coaches want feedback, all they have to do is pay attention. If things are not going according to plan, that's feedback on what needs to be done next. It takes incredible ownership to have this mentality.

PLAYBOOK REVIEW

COACH THE NEXT-PLAY MENTALITY

FACILITATE SELF-COACHING

ALIGN SELF-INTEREST

DEVELOP MIDDLE-LAYER MANAGEMENT

RETEACH

MODEL

REPRESENTING THE STANDARD

There was an NBA coach who hosted a holiday party for his team. Everyone wrote down their name on a sheet of paper and put it in a bowl. They played charades. The coach told me that it was so informative to watch a future Hall-of-Famer act him out because the way the player perceived him was not at all how he perceived himself.

What does that show?

In the NBA, players don't follow coaches, they evaluate them. The charades game offers perspective, it teaches you how your actions and words are being interpreted.

In the introduction I told you about the best lesson the Gonzaga men's basketball team learned from Mark Few. They answered, "How to be a good husband and how to be a good father." And how many conversations did Mark have with them about that?

None.

Mark believes that your actions are going to show where your values are.

I shared that story about Mark Few with his good friend, Billy Donovan. And here's Billy's take:

Billy Donovan
Chicago Bulls

If I was to walk around with a person for 48 hours and I was to look at that person's disciplines, I would be able to tell you what's important in that person's life.

If somebody wants to be in great shape and lose weight, I'll show you a disciplined person in terms of eating and working out. If I look at a guy and I see a marriage and his children are really, really important to him, you'll see a disciplined person in terms of the investments that are being made there.

The hard part is getting to a value system of what's really important to you, and then being disciplined in those things that are important to you.

What do you think about this line? "You can't see the label from inside the bottle."

When people observe you, they see you more clearly than you see you. If someone were to audit your normal activity, what would they say that you value? That response can provide great insight, because you're always modeling, whether you want to or not.

I asked Tim Corbin about the importance of modeling, and here's what he said:

Tim Corbin
Vanderbilt

Modeling is what people see. You can communicate however you wish, but if you don't follow up with your actions, then you're going to cross some signals.

When consistency is present, you don't cross as many signals. Bill Belichick is the physical manifestation of what consistency looks like. Here's one of my favorite examples of that.

Bill Belichick wrote a supportive letter to Donald Trump.

Trump read it on TV. Think about how that would go over in the locker room. It aired the week that the New England Patriots were playing the Seattle Seahawks. Here's how Bill navigated a press conference prior to the game. He opened up with a statement and then took questions:

Bill Belichick
New England Patriots

I have multiple friendships that are important to me. That's what that was about. It's not about politics, it's about football. We've got a huge game this week against a great football team, great organization, and that's where it all is going forward—on Seattle.

Reporter: *Coach, were you happy or annoyed that Trump read the letter?*

Belichick: *Seattle.*

Reporter: *Your team's always been good at keeping outside distractions on the outside. Given the nature of this presidential race—*

Belichick: *Seattle.*

Reporter: *Did you find it—*

Belichick: *Seattle.*

The reporters are asking him questions that try to trap his mind in the past. He pivots to what he's focused on—he's locked into the now. That sends a strong signal to his team. It takes a disciplined mind to do that.

Do you remember Bill Belichick's exchange with the reporter that I used in the beginning of the book?

Bill Belichick
New England Patriots

Reporter: *With all you've accomplished in your coaching career, what is left that you still want to accomplish?*

Belichick: *I'd like to go out and have a good practice today. That would be at the top of the list right now.*

This might be the simplest modeling tool that we can use. It was inspired by Bill's interaction with that reporter. I showed it to Mike Holder, the athletic director at Oklahoma State, and he said, "If I want my team to be in the moment then I need to be in the moment."

If I want my team to _____ then I need to _____.

When I asked Mike Holder, "How important is the example the coach sets?" Here's how he responded:

Mike Holder
Oklahoma State

It's everything. I think that's most prevalent when things go awry, when you fail, or when you face adversity.

For the coach to keep that in perspective and harness all the anger, disappointment, embarrassment, and push those down and reach out to the player to offer them what they need in that moment.

That's not what you're feeling. They're feeling the same thing. They're talking to themselves the same way. What they need is to hear a voice that lifts them up and inspires them.

Mike Holder tries to live by his line, "You are the physical manifestation of the standard."

What we've learned is that your example matters most when it's hardest. And if you want your team to be character driven then you need to be character driven.

Here's one way to use the modeling tool.

Think back to the Gonzaga thumbprint:

Imagine your team's logo in the center. What characteristics do you want your program to be defined by?

Here's a glossary that could help get you started:

PERFORMANCE SKILLS

Hardworking: Paying the price with effort
Competitive: Striving to be your best
Positive: Good and useful thinking
Focused: Eliminating distractions
Accountable: Taking responsibility for your actions
Courageous: Operating outside of your comfort zone
Resilient: Bouncing back from setbacks
Confident: Self-trusting
Enthusiastic: Expressing enjoyment
Disciplined: Self-regulating
Motivated: Having a strong purpose
Creative: Out-of-the-box thinking
Curious: Desiring to learn or understand

RELATIONAL SKILLS

Unselfish: Putting the team first
Honest: Telling the truth
Respectful: Showing consideration
Appreciative: Recognizing the good in someone or something
Humble: Distributing credit
Patient: Tolerating delay or struggle
Loyal: Showing allegiance
Trustworthy: Being reliable
Trustwilling: Relying on others
Encouraging: Giving confidence and support
Socially Aware: Understanding signals sent and received
Caring: Investing in the person
Empathetic: Sharing the feelings of others

What are the top five characteristics you want your team's DNA to be made up of?

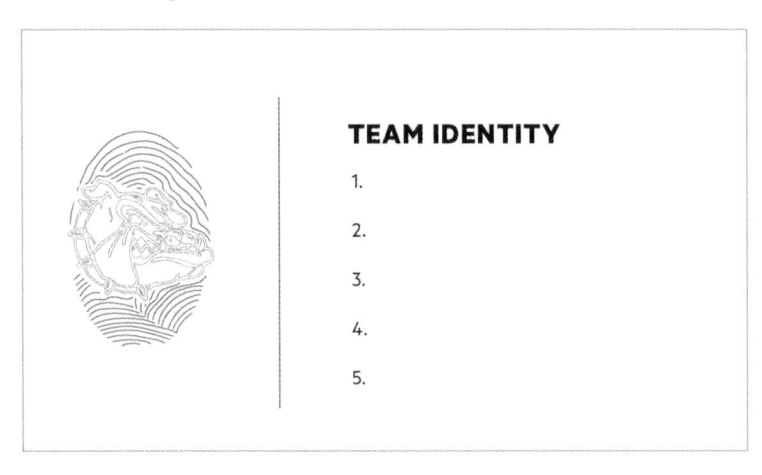

TEAM IDENTITY

1.
2.
3.
4.
5.

Then you plug those characteristics into this tool:

If I want my team to _____

then I need to _____

Your charge then becomes to model the behavior that represents the program's DNA. When you do that you avoid mixed signals. What's a mixed signal? When your words and actions don't align.

Think back to the clip from the movie *Old School*, when Will Ferrell is screaming, "We've got to keep our composure!" His words are in direct conflict with his actions.

I ask coaches, "What are the most common mixed signals you see in your profession?"

Here are a few that came to mind (next page):

WORDS		ACTIONS
"Be on time"	⚠	Comes late to meeting
"Be a great teammate"	⚠	Disrespects staff/family
"Take care of your body"	⚠	Doesn't exercise, eat well, or rest & recover
"Take accountability for your actions"	⚠	Plays the blame game
"Don't take it personally"	⚠	Emotionally reacts to feedback
"It's about the process"	⚠	Behavior fluctuates with outcomes

We could spend a lot of time on all of these, and this is obviously not an exhaustive list. Let's focus on the last two. "Don't take it personally" and "It's about the process."

I asked Chris Petersen, "What's something that you have taken personally?" He reflected:

Chris Petersen
Washington

When a player lets you down because they don't do what you ask them to do, and it's crossing the line.

You feel like you failed them. Or, "How could you do this to me?"

My wife says, "It's not about you. They weren't thinking about you."

I said (laughing), "That's the problem."

Chris' wife is thinking, "No, that's the problem!" This illustrates how easy it is to take things personally. It also illustrates why Hall-of-Fame football coach Bob Stoops would tell his younger self, "Don't personalize the mistakes made by others." That's so hard to do for most people.

A good friend of mine said, "The level to which you take things personally is directly related to the level you lack perspective in that moment."

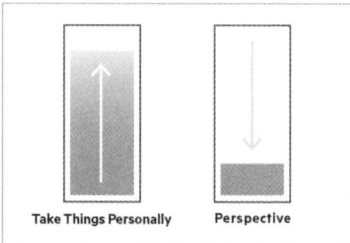

Take Things Personally | Perspective

Perspective can be hard to keep in a profession that has such a narrow view of success. That's why it's difficult to "focus on the process," because everyone around you is locked into the visible results.

That's something that former UCLA softball coach Sue Enquist talks about. She shared one of her biggest regrets:

Sue Enquist
UCLA

I have a lot of regrets. And one of them is actually throwing away a consolation trophy and getting caught. And when I look back at that, in the moment I realize that I didn't have clarity on some of the things that you should never, ever do. . . And [that there are] boundaries you should never cross.

Sue crossed a boundary that she wished she wouldn't have. What contributes to that? Think about this. In 2017, the University of Florida volleyball team lost in the national championship game. Head coach, Mary Wise, won National Coach of the Year. One week later, this happened in her hometown:

Mary Wise
Florida

This was maybe a week after the championship, and we were waiting outside at a restaurant. And a gentleman, probably older than me, walked by and he looked at me and you could see he recognized me. And went, "Hey! Oh. Oh, that match, that was really rough." And then he just walked away.

It's an all or nothing proposition. "You don't get the trophy. You failed." This is the lens that Mary Wise has been socialized through: →

It's hard to discern reality if you don't create a filter. Here's one way I do that with coaches.

(I explored this concept in depth in my book *What's Really Important* and at the 2018 What Drives Winning conference.)

I ask, "How does society measure your success (as a coach)?" Take a second to think about how you would answer that question. Here's an example of a response from a coach I was working with:

Wins/Losses
Championships
Rankings
Players at Next Level
Recruiting Class

After we are clear on how society measures their success, I ask them a different question about life in general. They write down the first ten things that come to mind in response to the question, "What's important to you?" Here's an example:

Family
Faith
Strong Character
Job Performance
Health
Friends
Relationships
Financial Security
Turning Boys into Men
My Staff

Think about your list. Would it be similar? Once a coach has their ten answers, I ask them to go back through and prioritize their top five. After we have the top five of what's most important to them, we stack society's scorecard right next to that:

What's important to you?	How does society measure success?
Faith	Wins / Losses
Family	Championships
Health	Rankings
Strong Character	Players at Next Level
Relationships	Recruiting Class

I then ask, "What do you notice?" How would you answer that? A lot of coaches will say, "You get so much positive reinforcement for the things on the right, it's easy to get out of whack with the things on the left."

What does that show us? Society's values are different from our personal values. If we don't understand that, that can lead to internal conflict and ultimately pull us away from the example that we are trying to model.

Sometimes you have to break down in order to break through. That's what happened to Vanderbilt baseball coach Tim Corbin. In the middle of a night in 2012, at 1:30 a.m., Tim was in the kitchen doing push-ups. He was struggling personally and professionally. His wife came down and asked, "What are you doing?" He looked at her in disbelief, and said, "I don't know."

She said, "If you don't find a different way to value what you're doing, you're going to die a miserable man."

That's why he created the classroom for his team. He started to teach his team the life lessons that he needed to learn. Think about this, when Tim is learning those lessons, what is he modeling? What it looks like to be the student. The classroom became a space where everybody could recalibrate each day.

An example of someone else outside of sports who needed to recalibrate was Dave Chappelle. Dave walked away from $50 million. As he reflected back on that experience in an interview with *Good Morning America*, here's the analogy that came to mind:

Dave Chappelle
Comedian

I watched one of these nature shows one time. And they were talking about how a bushman finds water when it's scarce. And they do what's called a salt trap—I didn't know this, but apparently baboons love salt.

So they put a lump of salt in a hole. And they wait for the baboon. The baboon comes, sticks his hand in the hole, grabs the salt, salt makes his hand bigger, and he's trapped. He can't get his hand out. Now if he's smart, all he does is let go of the salt, but the baboon doesn't want to let go of the salt.

Then the bushman comes, takes the baboon, throws him in the cage, and gives him all the salt he wants.

Then the baboon gets thirsty, the bushman lets him out of the cage, the first place the baboon runs to is water, bushman follows him, and they both drink to their fill. And in that analogy I felt like the baboon, but I was smart enough to let go of the salt.

What are you holding on to that you need to let go of? What's trapping you and keeping you from being your very best?

Most of my time spent individually with athletic directors, coaches, and athletes is spent on this concept: that the goal (what they're being paid to do) is in direct conflict with their purpose (their mission on earth). When your goal and purpose don't align, that can disrupt your internal experience. How do you combat that?

Here's an idea:

If your words and actions don't align, you're an **amateur**.

If your words/actions don't align with your thoughts, you're an **actor**.

If your words/actions/thoughts align, you're **authentic**.

There's strength and peace that comes with being authentic.

One of my favorite moments from the What Drives Winning conferences came at our inaugural event. It was the very first line of Dr. Jim Loehr's speech:

Dr. Jim Loehr
Performance Psychologist

I want to ask you a question. How important do you think it is that you know the reason behind what you're doing at any moment?

It's easy to blow through that question. But if you pause and think about it, it's profound.

It speaks to the intentionality of how you live your life. If you don't have intentionality, you just become a product of your environment and a prisoner to circumstance.

I was working with the University of Arkansas women's golf coach, Shauna Estes-Taylor. When Shauna was in college, she was an incredible golfer. After turning pro, she had to quit within a year due to rheumatoid arthritis. So she got into coaching.

She was observing her team and saw how emotionally attached they get to their scores. When they perform well, they feel good. When they don't, they feel bad.

Performance is where they're deriving their self-esteem from. Shauna began to think that if golf was taken away from them, they would really struggle.

She organized a team retreat and invited her friend, who was one of the strongest leaders that she knew, to speak. This friend was the president of a very prominent company. Here's what she presented to the team (next page):

> **Mission Statement**
> I invest and connect with people to make a difference: Coach, Lift, Role Model
>
> **#2 AWESOME WIFE**
> - Date's Booked
> - Lock step with kids
> - Active Listening
>
> **#1 ME & GOD!**
> Prayer Gratitude Meditation Exercise every morning
> Stay Present – This moment is the gift
> Recharge: Alone Time - In the woods
>
> **#3 FULLY ENGAGED MOM**
> - Words are encouraging
> - Book Family Time each week
> - Max: Leadership, Discipline, Friendship
> - Franki: Confident, Strong, Healthy
>
> **#4 SUPPORTIVE DAUGHTER/SISTER**
> - Family is 1st, 2nd, and last.
> - Connect weekly with blood
> - Never miss the important moments
>
> **#5 INSPIRING LEADER**
> - Connect & Inspire - Positive words & thoughts are magic
> - Lighthouse Leadership STRIDE 100% of the time
> - The Arena is where I play my best game – STAY IN!
>
> **Principles I live my life by...**
> LIVE the 4 Agreements = Be Impeccable with my word, Don't take it Personally, Don't make assumptions, Always give my best
> Today is the only gift you have – Carpe Diem!
> I am the peace and harmony that I want for my life, it starts with my thinking – keep it positive 100% of the time!!!
> I DEFINE and "Arena Player"
> Expect Chaos on the road to greatness – from breakdown comes breakthrough!

This is her framework on how she approaches life. She reviews this every morning.

At the top is her mission statement, how she wants to spend her time on earth.

There are five roles in order of importance. There are supporting actions under each role to make sure that she fulfills each one in a way that she would be proud of on her deathbed.

At the very bottom are the principles that she wants to approach each day with.

I think about coaches and how good they are at game planning for everybody else. But they don't plan for themselves.

Think about how your team would perform in a game without a game plan. That would be a disaster. Unfortunately, when this happens to coaches in real life, it becomes a tragedy.

This tool might be a starting point for you (next page):

MISSION STATEMENT

2 ROLE:
SUPPORTING ACTIONS:

3 ROLE:
SUPPORTING ACTIONS:

1 ROLE:
SUPPORTING ACTIONS:

4 ROLE:
SUPPORTING ACTIONS:

5 ROLE:
SUPPORTING ACTIONS:

CHARACTER-DRIVEN VALUES

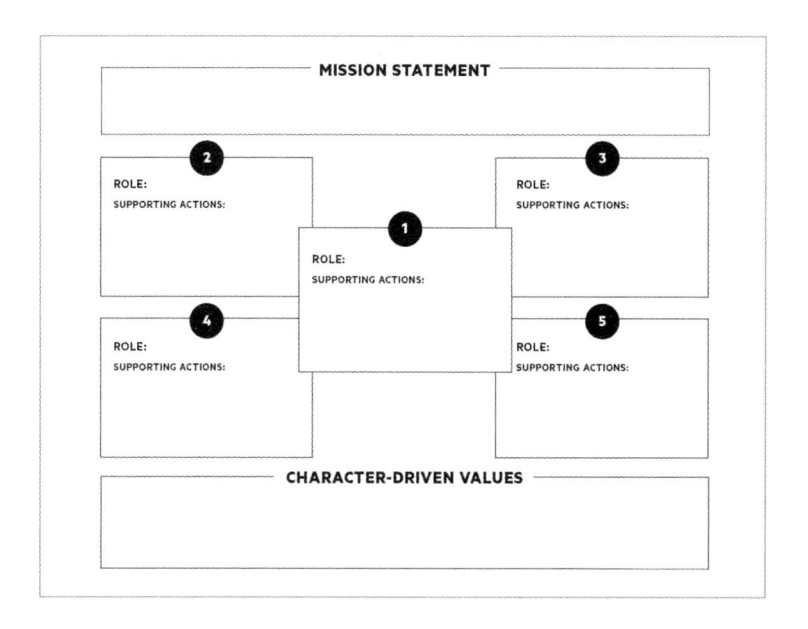

This can help bring you back to the big picture, a mental framework so you don't lose yourself through the busyness of the job. If you don't have something that's going to anchor you when the storm hits, it's easy to lose your way.

MODEL ROAD MAP

ALIGN WORDS & ACTIONS
Think about the identity of your program. What characteristics do you want your DNA to be made up of? Ask your staff and/or team, "What do I need to keep doing to support this with my actions?" "What do I need to stop doing?"

DEVELOP YOUR GAME PLAN
A coach would never show up to a game without a plan. Develop your plan. What's your mission on Earth? What are the roles you play? What are the supporting actions of those roles? What principles do you want to live by and make decisions based on? Practice that plan on a daily basis and let the job provide the challenge.

CREATE AN ACCOUNTABILITY SYSTEM
If you were coaching someone else on how to develop an accountability system to audit this road map, what would you tell them? What kind of structure would you set up to make sure that you stay on track? Here's my challenge to you: Take your own advice.

Author's Note

A coach shared with me what he felt drove his success. He said, "I feel like I've learned how to control my team in order to suppress other teams." That's a dark space to live in. Especially when that approach has been positively reinforced by so many wins and a celebrated Hall-of-Fame career. It can leave you asking a lot of questions about life.

Many coaches that I've observed have leveraged highly controlled environments to produce the consistent behavior necessary to win at a high level. But nobody really feels good about it. That's why it took me so long to write this book. I didn't want to study how people used their power to force control. I wanted to write a different book. Once I understood how to do that, I decided to take this journey.

I asked a successful coach, "What's the best way to change undesired behavior?" He laughed, "The best? Or the fastest?"

When there are clear power dynamics, you can use a set of tactics that work on a short-term basis to produce results. But if you choose that approach, that's a miserable way to spend your time on Earth. It's a hollow path toward empty W's.

That's why I love the NBA. That environment requires a higher form of management. If you strip the coach of his power, he has to rely on logic, listening, and learning how to meet people where they are. That job becomes about winning influence. The respect is earned, not given, in that league.

I think about the coaches who clearly have power over their team, but choose to win influence instead. That rare group is motivated to find their next level as leaders. Their example influences people to discover their best.

I strongly believe in a more diverse, progressive approach toward coaching. I hope this book has helped you think through how you define, manage, and model your expectations as a coach in a way that you would ultimately want to reflect in your life.

WATCH THE WORKSHOP
WDWE.WhatDrivesWinning.com

Chris Petersen
Washington

Brett Ledbetter
Performance Consultant